Part of the "NEARBY" series of books.

THE FIRE STATION

Part of the "Nearby" series of books.

BY: DA BUTLER

Brothers Arthur and Andy woke up early and came downstairs for breakfast. As they sat at the table their mommy said "boys, I have a special surprise for you today!"

Arthur and Andy love surprises!

"Mommy, mommy, what is it?" Andy squealed. "Yes, mommy, please tell us," shouted Arthur.

"Today we will be walking down the street to visit our local fire station."

Arthur and Andy hopped off of their chairs and jumped up and down in the kitchen. They were so excited!

"Go and get ready boys, we are leaving in ten minutes!"

The boys ran to their rooms, brushed their teeth and met mommy at the front door.

As they walked down the sidewalk to the fire station, Arthur and Andy thought about all of the questions they want to ask the firefighters when they arrive. What questions would you ask?

When they arrived at the fire station mommy said hello to a friendly looking firefighter.

"Hello boys, my name is Frank, I'm going to show you around the station and answer any questions that you have."

Arthur and Andy both replied "Hi Frank!"

Frank told Arthur and Andy that the firefighters were in the kitchen cleaning up after having their breakfast.

Frank explained that everyone helps at the fire station when they are not fighting a fire or helping with another emergency. Everyone cleans the station, the fire trucks and the equipment. It is very important to make sure that everything is ready for when they need it.

Andy noticed the fire pole and asked Frank if they could slide down it. Frank replied, "unfortunately Andy, the pole is for firefighters only. We use the pole to reach the ground floor as fast as we can when there is an emergency."

Arthur asked Frank if the firefighters live here at the station.

"That's a great question, Arthur. Our firefighters work for 24 hours straight. That's a whole day and night. They eat and sleep here . When the alarm goes off and they need to go to a call, they are rested, fed and ready to work."

Mommy, Arthur, Andy and Frank walked down the stairs so Frank could show them the firefighter's uniforms.

Frank explained that a firefighter's uniform has many jobs to do. They have a helmet to protect their head, pants and a jacket that helps to keep away the heat. They also have thick leather gloves to safely handle hot objects and thick, waterproof rubber boots.

Mommy, Arthur and Andy thanked Frank for showing them around the fire station. As they were about to leave Frank said, "I have one more surprise for you two boys."

Arthur and Andy jumped up and down, "we love surprises!"

Frank walked them to the firetruck and opened the door. "Hop up boys, have a look inside."

They boys were so happy to be able to sit inside the firetruck. They tried on helmets and were allowed to push the button to start the siren. It was so loud! This was the best day ever.

On their walk home, Arthur and Andy talked about all that they had learned. They liked the uniforms and the fire pole but most of all they loved the firetruck because they were allowed to sit in it and see how everything works.

"I want to be a firefighter," said Arthur.
"I want to be a firefighter too," said Andy.

Both boys fell asleep dreaming about being firefighters when they grow up!

More titles in the NEARBY series:

The Backyard
The Farm
The Library

Other DA BUTLER titles:

My Glasses
Freckles!
My Daddy
Kindness
Forever Friend
The New Baby

www.ingramcontent.com/pod-product-compliance
Lightning Source LLC
Chambersburg PA
CBHW041403010526
44107CB00015B/1061